Teaching Tunes
Audio CD and Mini-Books Set
FAVORITE SONGS

by Dr. Jean Feldman

S C H O L A S T I C
PROFESSIONAL BOOKS

New York ♪ Toronto ♪ London ♪ Auckland ♪ Sydney ♪ Mexico City ♪ New Delhi ♪ Hong Kong ♪ Buenos Aires

Dedication

This book is dedicated to the parents, grandparents, teachers, and children of all ages who have kept these nursery rhymes and songs alive through the years. The enduring magic of these tunes is a reminder of the joy they can give children today!

It is my hope that the children who learn these songs will continue to pass them on to future generations.

Acknowledgments

Mark Dye has given my songs music and wings! I thank him for his musical genius, creativity, and commitment to FUN!

Jennifer Hiltz, Felitsa Kardassis, and Amy Weaver have added "childlike magic" to these songs. Thank you for your voices and your smiles.

I thank Liza Charlesworth for seeing the value in these books and for her dedication to giving children a reason to sing and read!

Danielle Blood has nurtured this project and brought it to life! I thank her for her enthusiasm, insight, leadership, and talents.

Thanks to Lynn Mondello Caggiano for editing the activities with great care.

Maxie Chambliss's gifted hand has added the delightful and charming illustrations!

Thanks to the creative and thoughtful work of Ellen Matlach Hassell, who designed the book's interior, and Josué Castilleja and Kelli Thompson, who designed the cover.

And thanks to my mother, teachers, scout leaders, camp counselors, students, and colleagues who have shared these wonderful songs and ideas with me!

Music reminds us all that it is still a wonderful world and we have a lot to sing about!

Cover design by Josué Castilleja and Kelli Thompson

Cover and interior illustrations by Maxie Chambliss

Interior design by Ellen Matlach Hassell for Boultinghouse & Boultinghouse, Inc.

Edited by Lynn Mondello Caggiano

Product ISBN: 0-439-30591-8

Book ISBN: 0-439-30592-6

Contents

Introduction

I recently heard someone comment, "We are so busy trying to give our children things we didn't have, that we fail to give them what we did have." How true! It is my joy and privilege to share an important part of my childhood with you.

I was a lucky little girl. I didn't have a television, computer, or VCR when I was young, but I did have my record player with its plastic red and yellow records. I can remember sitting on the floor singing "London Bridge," "Mary Had a Little Lamb," and "Hey Diddle Diddle" time and again. My mother didn't know it then, but that was one of the best things she could have done to nurture my developing literacy skills. These old songs and nursery rhymes are as important today as they were 50 or 100 years ago. Current research suggests that one of the best ways to develop reading skills is through rhyming activities, such as songs and chants (NAEYC, 2000).

Additionally, we now know that lap reading and the number of books children own are primary predictors of reading success. That's why Teaching Tunes books help create win-win learning situations. Not only can you use them in your classroom but children can also take them home to share with their families. As part of our musical heritage, these tunes connect past, present, and future generations through story and rhyme.

Top 10 Reasons to Use This Book

♪ **Motivate children to read.** These songs and mini-books motivate children to read and show them that reading is fun. Once they learn the songs, kids can read along in their own mini-books. Before long, they will be reading!

♪ **Build phonological awareness.** The rhythm, rhyme, and alliteration of these songs help children develop phonological awareness, an essential step in learning to read.

♪ **Help kids make the connection between the spoken word and print.** These songs reinforce the idea that "what I say can be written down, and what is written down I can read."

♪ **Help children learn to track and use picture clues.** The mini-books reinforce the concept of following a line of print from left to right. Children also learn to use the picture clues to help them read the text.

♪ **Tap into diverse learning styles.** The combination of songs and mini-books works well for a variety of learning styles: There is singing for auditory learners, text and illustrations for visual learners, and suggested movements for kinesthetic learners.

♪ **Reinforce important reading concepts.** Use these songs to reinforce important reading concepts such as word families, initial consonants, vowel sounds, and more. The more kids sing, the more they'll learn!

♪ **Provide take-home books.** Many children do not have access to books at home. These reproducible mini-books are a great way to help children build their own libraries. The books also provide a link between school and home, encouraging families to take part in the learning process and spend quality time together.

♪ **Enhance the classroom community.** Singing is a wonderful group activity that builds a sense of community and cooperation. No matter what their reading level, all children will have fun joining in.

♪ **Develop small-motor skills.** Children build small-motor skills as they cut, color, and assemble the book pages in numerical order.

♪ **Have fun!** Children learn best when they're having fun. So start singing, smiling, reading, and learning!

People sing because they're happy, and they're happy because they sing! My hope is that these books will bring much happiness to your classroom. For additional information, please visit **www.drjean.org**.

Keep on singing!

Dr. Jean Feldman

How to Use This Book

Teaching Tunes Audio CD and Mini-Books Set: Favorite Songs is the fourth book in the Teaching Tunes series, following *Teaching Tunes Audiotape and Mini-Books Set: Basic Concepts, Teaching Tunes Audiotape and Mini-Books Set: Early Phonics,* and *Teaching Tunes Audio CD and Mini-Books Set: Nursery Rhymes.* These mini-books and songs can be integrated into any reading program and used in a number of ways. The songs and mini-books provide opportunities to teach a variety of reading skills, such as tracking a line of print, turning the page, using picture clues, identifying letters and high-frequency words, and sounding out words. They are designed for flexible use with individual children, partners, small groups, or the whole class.

Send-Home Mini-Books

Children love to share these songs and mini-books with their families. Send home a letter to families explaining the purpose of the mini-books and encouraging them to reinforce reading skills at home. (See the sample letter to families on page 9. Frequent communication with parents will help them guide children's at-home reading efforts.) Children can create their own personal "libraries" in which to store their mini-books. Ask each child to bring to school an empty cereal box or other container. Let them decorate their containers with wallpaper, wrapping paper, and other materials. As children make their mini-books, they can store them in their libraries.

Group Reading

Introduce the songs to children before making the mini-books. (See How to Make the Mini-Books, page 8.) In this way, children will become familiar with the song lyrics and will be more motivated to read the books. To reinforce reading skills, write the song lyrics on sentence strips to place in a pocket chart. Try some of these suggestions for small- or large-group reading experiences:

♪ **Shared Reading** Model how to track a line of print, turn the page, use picture clues, and so forth.

♪ **Guided Reading** Relate pictures to print, point out letters and high-frequency words, and integrate with other reading and writing skills. Use the overhead projector to display words and songs. Circle or highlight rhyming words, punctuation, and anything else you would like students to notice.

♪ **Choral Reading** Read together as you point to the words. (See page 7 for pointer ideas.)

♪ **Shadow Reading** You read a line and then children repeat it.

♪ **Take a Turn** You read a line, children read the next line, and so on.

♪ **Magic Word** Select a particular word in the text. Every time you come to the magic word, children clap their hands, shout the word, or whisper the word.

♪ **Partner Reading** Have children read with a partner and take turns reading or singing the words together.

Learning Centers

There are a number of ways that you can use the songs and mini-books in learning centers. Place the CD and mini-books in a listening center so that children will have the opportunity to review the

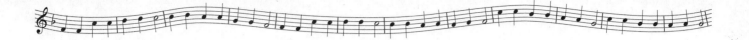

songs they enjoy most. Encourage partners to visit the listening center and sing the songs together. They can take turns singing alternate pages, or they can sing the whole song together.

Sing-along mini-books are just one way to present song lyrics to children and build early literacy skills. Research suggests that literacy skills are enhanced when children are exposed to multiple copies of familiar text in different mediums. Here are more ideas that are perfect for learning centers:

♪ **Big Books** Create oversized books to accompany the mini-books. You might use poster board cut in half, large paper grocery sacks, tagboard, or other materials. Use large handwriting or type for the lyrics. Have children illustrate the text.

♪ **Tag-Along Books** These are books that children can tote! Make a big book and punch two holes through the left side. Attach a pipe cleaner or piece of yarn for a handle. (To display these, simply hang them with clothespins on a clothesline.)

♪ **Book Puzzles** Cut apart the book pages and trim off the page numbers. Glue the pages onto 5- by 6-inch sheets of construction paper. Invite children to arrange the pages in sequential order. (Store book puzzles in resealable plastic bags.)

♪ **Sing-Along Notebook** Make a song sheet for each mini-book. Have children illustrate the song sheets, and then store them in a three-ring binder. Use the songbook to entertain children during transitions, or let children take turns using it as they lead a class sing-along. Invite other classes to visit, and let your students teach them the songs as well.

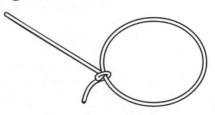

Using Pointers

Encourage children to use pointers to help them make the connection between the printed word and spoken word. Have children place a pointer on each word as they read or sing it. Before reading together as a group, give each student a pointer and do the following fun finger exercise. Have kids follow your movements with their own pointers as you say:

Let's get the pointers ready! Up!	Hold your pointer up.
Down!	Hold your pointer down.
All around!	Wiggle your pointer around.
Attention!	Hold your pointer up straight.
On the word!	Point to the first word in the book.

Here are a few kinds of pointers that children will enjoy using:

♪ **Wiggly Eye** Have each child glue a movable eye to the end of a craft stick. Challenge each child to "Keep your eye on the word!"

♪ **Magic Pointer** Have each child dip the end of a craft stick in glue and then in glitter.

♪ **Plastic Fingernails** Give each child a plastic fingernail to glue to a craft stick. (Plastic fingernails are often sold around Halloween.)

♪ **Finger Puppet** Cut off the fingers of several pairs of inexpensive light-colored cloth work gloves. Give each child one finger to decorate with fine-tip markers. Encourage kids to name their "finger buddies" and use them as pointers when they read.

♪ **Seasonal Pointers** Glue small seasonal erasers, stickers, or small toys to craft sticks or straws. (Action figures found in children's meals at fast-food restaurants work well.)

♪ **Pipe Cleaner Monocle** Twist the end of a pipe cleaner into a circle as shown to make a monocle. Children can use it as they read or to focus on particular words.

Large pointers work well for reading together as a group. Copy the song lyrics onto sentence strips to use in a pocket chart. You might also make an oversized copy of the mini-books out of poster board or brown paper bags. Then use one of the following pointers as you read or sing together.

♪ **Magic Wand** Wrap aluminum foil around a cardboard tube from a pants hanger. Dip one end in glue and then in glitter.

♪ **Stuffed Glove** Take a cloth work glove and color the tips with a red marker to look like fingernails. Stuff the glove with polyester fiberfill or cotton. Use a pipe cleaner to attach the glove to a paint stirrer or other stick. Use a glue gun to secure the glove in place. Then glue down four of the fingers, leaving the index finger pointing up.

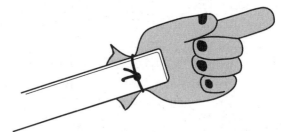

How to Make the Mini-Books

These mini-books are designed for double-sided copying. If your machine does not have a double-sided function, make copies of the title page first. Then place these copies into the machine's paper tray. Next, make a copy of the second page so that page 2 copies directly behind the title page. (For 16-page books, copy the pages so that page 6 copies directly behind page 5.) For variety, copy some books on light-colored paper. Show children how to assemble their mini-books by following these steps:

1. Cut the page(s) in half along the solid line.
2. **For an 8-page book,** place pages 4/5 on top of pages 2/7, as shown.

   For a 16-page book, place pages 8/9 on top, followed by pages 6/11, pages 4/13, and pages 2/15, as shown.

3. Fold the pages in half along the dotted line.
4. Check to be sure that the pages are in the correct numerical order. Then staple the pages together along the mini-book's spine.
5. Encourage children to personalize their books by coloring them with crayons, markers, or colored pencils.

Create your own mini-books using poems or other songs that children enjoy. Happy singing and reading!

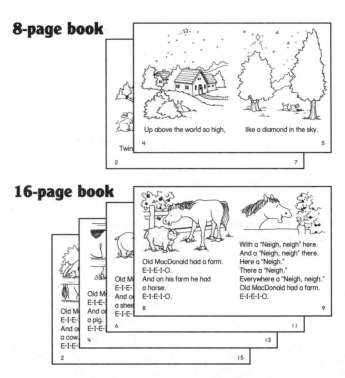

8-page book

16-page book

Date _____

Dear Family,

Our class is learning songs that help children develop early reading skills. Each song comes with a mini-book that provides the song lyrics and illustrations that support the text. When children have learned the songs, they can read along in their mini-books. The rhyme and rhythm of the songs make them fun to sing—and help children as they are learning to read.

Your child will be excited to share these songs and mini-books with you at home. Most of the songs are set to simple, familiar tunes that are easy to learn. Please set aside time to enjoy these songs and books together. Here are some specific suggestions to make the most of this experience:

♪ Encourage your child to point to the words as he or she reads or sings them.

♪ Sing along with your child.

♪ Ask your child questions about the pictures. How do the pictures help your child know what the words are?

♪ Help your child decorate a shoe box or cereal box in which he or she can store the books.

♪ Take out the books from time to time and review them with your child.

♪ Encourage your child by commenting on how his or her reading is improving.

♪ Have fun! Follow your child's lead.

♪ Teach your child songs you remember from your own childhood.

Thank you for sharing this experience with your child.

Sincerely,

_____

Directions and Activities

Twinkle, Twinkle, Little Star

Purpose

Children build phonemic awareness by manipulating onset and rime patterns. Children develop awareness of sound-symbol correspondence as they track lines of print from left to right.

Directions

Sing "Twinkle, Twinkle, Little Star." Ask children if they've heard this song before and who taught it to them. Explain that there are some songs that children have been singing for a long, long time. Their parents, grandparents, and great-grandparents probably sang "Twinkle, Twinkle, Little Star" when they were children! Tell children that they will make their own songbooks that they can take home and share with their families. Pass out copies of the mini-book pages and show children how to assemble the books. When they are finished, play the song and encourage children to sing along. Follow along in the text with your finger, pointing to each word in your book as it's sung.

Have children identify words in the song that rhyme. Use magnetic letters to spell the word *star*. Leave a slight space between the onset (beginning sound) and the rime (vowel and letters that follow). Read the word aloud a few times, emphasizing the onset and rime. Then push the letters together and say the word as one unit, without exaggeration. Together, slowly blend the letter sounds in *star*. Ask children to predict what might happen if you

took away /st/ and replaced it with /j/. Demonstrate this with the magnetic letters. Guide children as they blend the sounds to make the new word. Continue making new words by replacing the onset with consonants such as *b, t, c,* and *f*. Repeat this activity using the base word *sky*; replace *sk* with *tr, cr, fl,* and *b*.

Activities

♪ Give each child a craft stick and a paper star. Have children glue their star to the end of the stick to create a "starry" pointer. Encourage children to use the stick to point to words as they follow along. For an added twinkle, use glow-in-the-dark stars.

♪ Guide children as they listen for the rhyming words in the following verse:

Star light, star bright,
first star I see tonight.
I wish I may, I wish I might,
have my wish come true tonight!

♪ Have children wave their star pointers when they hear rhyming words.

♪ Teach children how to catch a shooting star! Explain that when they do something that makes them proud, they should reach up, catch an imaginary star, and place it on their heart.

♪ Explain to children that stars are far, far away, and that even though sometimes our dreams and goals also seem far, far away, we shouldn't give up. That's why when we encourage people to follow their dreams, we often say, "Reach for the stars!" Encourage children to think of their dreams and goals and to draw themselves achieving those goals. Some goals might include becoming a firefighter, learning to read, or learning to tie shoes. Give each child a sheet

of paper with a large star drawn on it (you might make photocopies in advance). Instruct children to cut out the stars and draw a picture of themselves accomplishing their goal. Have children dictate a sentence about their pictures. To create star mobiles, punch holes in the top of the stars and hang them from clothes hangers with yarn. Add glitter or sparkle dust if desired.

The Muffin Man

Purpose

Children increase phonemic awareness by creating alliterative word patterns. Children identify periods and question marks.

Directions

Discuss why is it important to know your address; ask children if they know theirs. Tell them you know a song about the Muffin Man, whose address is Drury Lane. Sing the song for children. Ask if they've heard the song before. Invite children to join you as you sing the song again. Write the words to the song on an easel or chart paper and point to each word as it's sung.

Discuss the purpose of punctuation marks. Explain that when you ask a question, you put a question mark at the end of the sentence. When you answer a question, you put a period at the end. Sing the question in the song ("Do you know the muffin man…?"). Invite children to sing the answer ("Yes, we know the muffin man…"). Switch roles if desired.

Distribute the mini-book pages for children to assemble. Ask children to find a question mark in their books. Then have them find a period.

Activities

♪ Have children repeat the words *muffin* and *man*. Discuss how these words are alike. Can they think of other words that begin with /m/? Write suggestions on an easel or poster paper, underlining /m/. Ask volunteers to illustrate the list.

♪ Have children compose new verses with their names and addresses. Encourage them to think of adjectives that start with the same letter as their names. For example, "Do you know Silly Sarah, Silly Sarah, Silly Sarah? Do you know Silly Sarah, who lives on Maple Street?"

♪ Help children learn their address by having them sing it to the tune of "The Muffin Man." For example, sing, "325 Oak Street, Oak Street, Oak Street. 325 Oak Street is where Oscar lives."

♪ Have children make their own a spyglass by twisting the end of a pipe cleaner in a loop. Encourage children to use their spyglass to find question marks and periods in big books, pocket charts, library books, and so on.

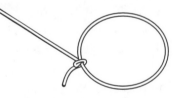

♪ Invite kids to move with the groove to learn punctuation! Have children clap when they see a period and snap when they see a question mark. Read big books and other selections where children can practice identifying punctuation marks. You could even have them jump up when they see an exclamation point!

♪ Make muffins from a mix and eat them for snack. (**Safety Note:** Some children have food allergies or other dietary restrictions. Be sure to obtain a food restriction list from families before proceeding with any food-related activities.)

Itsy Bitsy Spider

Purpose
Children recognize opposites.

Directions
Sing the song to children, using the motions below:

The itsy bitsy spider went up the waterspout.
> Press your right index finger to your left thumb. Keep them together as you move your right thumb up to touch your left index finger. Continue rotating fingers and thumbs, moving your hands up to similuate climbing.

Down came the rain and washed the spider out.
> Spread fingers and bring them down as if raining.

Out came the sun and dried up all the rain.
> Make circle around your head with your arms.

And the itsy bitsy spider went up the spout again.
> Rotate thumbs and fingers up.

Teach children the finger actions and invite them to sing along. Distribute copies of the mini-book pages to assemble and color. Ask children to look for the picture of the spider crawling up. Then ask them to find the page where the spider is being washed down the waterspout. Explain that words that mean completely different things are called opposites. Provide examples such as *happy* and *sad* and *little* and *big*. Say, "The opposite of *up* would be . . . ," and encourage students to guess the answer. Brainstorm together other opposites and have children act them out.

Activities...

♪ Create new verses incorporating opposites. You might include the *teensy weensy spider* sung in a high, squeaky voice and accompanied by tiny motions, and the *great big, giant spider* sung in a loud voice and accompanied by large, exaggerated motions.

♪ Replace the spider with student names—for example, "Jana Lee went up the waterspout . . ."

♪ Instruct children to form a circle and place their hands on the shoulders of the person in front of them. Then tell them to drop their hands to their sides. Explain that they will learn to give a "spider massage." Have them perform the following movements as they sing:

The itsy bitsy spider went up the waterspout.
> Crawl fingers up the back of the person in front of them.

Down came the rain and washed the spider out.
> Gently scratch the person's back.

Out came the sun and dried up all the rain.
> Rub the person's back in circular motions.

And the itsy bitsy spider went up the spout again.
> Crawl fingers up the person's back.

♪ Have spider sandwiches for snack. Use a large plastic cup to cut circles out of two bread slices. Spread jelly in between the bread circles. Use raisins to make eyes and a mouth on top of the sandwich. Insert eight pretzel sticks or carrot sticks in the sides for legs. (**Safety Note:** Some children have food allergies or other dietary restrictions. Be sure to obtain a food restriction list from families before proceeding with any food-related activities.)

It's Raining, It's Pouring

Purpose
Children review *-ing* verbs.

Directions
Ask whether anyone has been in a big rainstorm or thunderstorm and have children describe their experiences. Explain that sometimes when it rains very hard, people say, "It's pouring." Ask children

what they think this means. Sing "It's Raining, It's Pouring" encouraging children to join in. Pass out mini-book pages for children to assemble. Have them look at the pictures and describe what is happening. Sing the song several times as children track the words in their books.

Write *raining, pouring,* and *snoring* on the chalkboard. Establish how these words are similar and circle the *-ing* for emphasis. Let children apply the *-ing* ending to other words. Ask, for example, "What would happen if I put *-ing* at the end of *walk*? What would the new word be?" Provide additional examples. On the chalkboard or on chart paper, write verbs that you can add *-ing* to without doubling the final consonant or dropping the silent *e* (*jump, look, work, turn, hang, act,* and so on). Let children come up and add *-ing* to the end of each word. Have them read the newly created word and use it in a sentence.

Activities

♪ Provide children with highlighters and old magazines or other materials that they can write on. Have children look for and highlight verbs ending in *-ing*.

♪ Using the reproducible on page 20, children can create new words by adding *-ing*. Have children cut out the word boxes and the *-ing* boxes. As a class, combine a word and an ending, then read aloud the new word. Glue the word in a space. Repeat these steps until all words have been made.

♪ Make rainy pictures! After kids draw with water-soluble markers, have them squirt their pictures with a water-filled spray bottle. Hang to dry.

♪ Brainstorm fun things to do when it rains. Write ideas on a classroom easel or sentence strips. Using these suggestions, write a story together about a rainy day.

♪ Encourage children to think analytically. What would happen if it didn't rain? What happens if it rains too much? What happens to puddles after it rains?

Yankee Doodle

Purpose
Children segment and count syllables.

Directions
Invite children on a pony ride! Have children stand up, put one foot in front of the other, tighten their fists in front of their body as if holding reins, and rock back and forth as you sing "Yankee Doodle." Next, have children face a partner, hold hands, and rock back and forth as they sing. Repeat several times, and then distribute mini-books for assembly.

Explain that syllables capture the beat of a word. Say, "We can clap to help measure the number of syllables we hear." Using *yankee* and *doodle* as examples, exaggerate the syllables and clap simultaneously. Have children repeat and count the number of syllables they hear. Together, clap the syllables in each of the following words: *went, to, town, macaroni.* Using other words from the verse (*town, riding, pony, feather,* and so on), ask children to clap out syllables on their own. Provide guidance as necessary. Finally, repeat the entire song, clapping out the syllables in each word.

Activities

♪ Clap the number of syllables in each child's name. Have children take turns choosing objects around the classroom. As a group, say the name of the object while clapping out the syllables.

♪ Play music and have children practice keeping a steady beat by clapping, marching, hopping, skipping, galloping, and making other motions. Choose a variety of music, from classical to country and jazz.

♪ Let children make their own stick ponies. Begin by rolling four open sheets of newspaper lengthwise. Tape together to form a pole. To make the head, draw the face on the bottom of a

brown paper lunch bag. Glue two paper triangles for the ears. Stuff the bag with newspaper, then attach with masking tape to one end of the newspaper pole, as shown. Invite kids to practice galloping around the classroom or on the playground as you sing "Yankee Doodle."

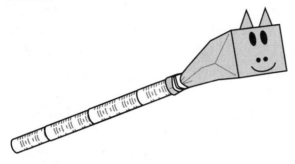

♪ Distribute the reproducible feather on page 21. Instruct children to color and cut out their feather. Glue craft feathers onto each feather if desired. Fit a strip of oaktag or colored construction paper (approximately 2 by 22 inches) around each child's head as a headband; fasten with tape. Have children wear their Yankee Doodle hats as they sing the song.

♪ Ask children how Yankee Doodle traveled to town. (*on a pony*) How else could he have traveled? Make a web of different types of transportation Yankee Doodle could have used.

Three Little Kittens

Purpose
Children retell a story in sequential order. Children identify basic story elements (problem, solution, and characters).

Directions
Invite children to share stories about a time that they lost something. What happened? How did they feel? Did anyone else become upset because they lost something? Tell students that they will learn a song about a group of kittens that lost their mittens.

After singing the song, ask children to recall what happened first in the story. What did the mother do? What happened next? How does the story end? Have volunteers act out the parts of the mother and three kittens as you sing the song again.

Pass out the mini-book pages for children to assemble. Discuss the concepts of problem, solution, and story characters. After singing the song again, ask children to identify the characters in the story. Then ask them what the problem was and how it was solved. Invite children to speculate what might happen next.

Activities ....

♪ Make copies of the mittens on page 22. Color or cut out the mittens from construction paper, wallpaper, or fabric (make sure that each pair of mittens matches). Children can play a matching game of Concentration by arranging the mittens facedown and taking turns finding matching pairs. Or place the mittens in a basket and have children take turns choosing mittens until they have found all the pairs.

♪ Read aloud *The Mitten* by Jan Brett.

♪ Play the Mystery Kittens game. Choose one child to play the role of mother or father cat and ask that child to leave the room. Then choose three students to be the kittens. The three kittens begin meowing softly while the other children in the room remain silent. When the mother or father cat returns to the room, he or she tries to find the kittens by figuring out who is meowing.

Row, Row, Row Your Boat

Purpose
Children distinguish between *fast* and *slow*. Children practice keeping a steady beat.

Directions
Have children sit on the floor, extend their feet, and rock back and forth as they pretend to row a boat. Sing the song as they row. Next, sing the song quickly and have them rock to the beat again. Finally, sing the song slowly as children rock slowly.

Give children mini-book pages to assemble. Sing the song again, guiding children as they track the words with their fingers. Ask children what they think it means to say "Life is but a dream." Invite children to share their own dream and then draw a picture of it.

Activities...

♪ Sing other familiar songs quickly and slowly. Play different styles and selections of music and have children identify the music as fast or slow. Invite children to name fast- and slow-moving animals.

♪ Children may enjoy rowing with a partner. Have pairs of students sit on the floor facing each other, with the soles of their shoes touching and their knees bent. Partners should grasp each other's hands and move back and forth at the waist as they sing the song.

♪ Discuss several modes of water transportation and the ways they differ (rowboats, sailboats, motorboats, and so on). Make a class poster with drawings or photos of each of these boats.

♪ Let children design their own boats to float in the water table or in a tub of water. Provide them with wooden or plastic blocks, wooden or plastic spools, foam, foil, clay, paper, and toothpicks. Provide an opportunity for children to share their boats with the class.

♪ Make ocean sandwiches for snack. Add a small amount of blue food coloring to whipped cream cheese. Spread it on half a bagel. Add miniature fish crackers on top, and enjoy! (**Safety Note:** Some children have food allergies or other dietary restrictions. Be sure to obtain a food restriction list from families before proceeding with any food-related activities.)

London Bridge

Purpose
Children recognize signs and learn about the purpose of signs.

Directions
Teach children a game to play as they learn the words to this song. Choose two children to form the bridge—one child will be silver and the other gold. Have the two children face each other, hold hands, and lift their arms to form a bridge. Instruct the rest of the class to line up single file and walk under the bridge as everyone sings the song. When you reach "…my fair lady," the children who are the bridge drop their hands down and catch the student who happens to be under the bridge. The students who are the bridge continue to hold hands and gently rock the person in the middle back and forth as you sing the rest of the song. At the end of the song, the child in the middle chooses either silver or gold and stands behind that child. The game continues until everyone has been caught and is standing behind silver or gold.

Pass out the mini-book pages for children to assemble. Read the words on each page and discuss the pictures. Help children make the connection between the illustrations and the text. Sing the song together as children track the words on each page.

Activities...................................

♪ Invite children to find the sign that says "London Bridge." What are some other signs they can read? Discuss signs children have seen around school or in the community. As a class, walk around the school, taking inventory of the different signs posted. Have children illustrate and label the signs they saw.

♪ Ask children if they've heard of London or know where it is. Locate London on a map or a globe. Explain that the original London Bridge is no longer in London. Show children pictures of other well-known sites in London, such as Big Ben, the Tower Bridge, and Trafalgar Square. Challenge children to do at-home research with their parents to see what else they can find out about London. Can they find out what happened to the original London Bridge? You might be surprised! (It was dismantled and reconstructed in Lake Havasu City, Arizona.)

♪ Using the Internet, explore today's weather in London. Discuss ways London's climate may differ from the climate where you live.

♪ Have children build a bridge in the block center. They might also enjoy constructing bridges with toothpicks and foam.

Ring Around the Rosie

Purpose
Children will identify and create compound words.

Directions
Have children stand up in a circle, hold hands, and walk in a circle as you sing the song. When you reach "…we all fall down," model how to gently squat to the ground. Stand up and sing the second verse of the song, ending by standing on your toes. Ask children whether they've heard this song before and whether anyone knows a different version of the song. Sing the song while you walk in a circle several more times, then pass out copies of the mini-book pages for children to assemble.

Write *upstairs* and *downstairs* on the chalkboard or on chart paper. Ask children if they recognize two small words in each of these big words. Explain that words made up of two smaller words are called compound words. Choose a child to circle the smaller words in each. Write several other compound words on the board, such as *cupcake, football, bedroom, doghouse,* and *sailboat.* Ask children to circle the smaller words in each. Have them think of other compound words to add to the list. Continue orally by saying two smaller words and asking students to name the compound word. For example, prompt children with *snow* and *man.*

Activities...

♪ Make compound-word puzzles. Write compound words on paper plates, cut between the words, and shuffle the pieces. Then have children match appropriate words and read the compound words they have created.

♪ Ask children to identify how the words *ring* and *rosie* are alike. Have them name other words that begin with /r/.

♪ Show children how to draw a rosie rainbow ring with crayons. First, draw a red circle and then draw an orange circle around the red one. Continue in the same way with yellow, green, blue, and purple. You might review other shapes by having children make rosie squares, triangles, and so on.

Did You Ever See a Lassie?

Purpose

Children segment and sequence the sounds they hear in words. Children review beginning and final consonant sounds.

Directions

Determine whether children are familiar with the word *lassie*. Explain that Lassie is the name of a dog on television, but it's also the word for "little girl" in Scotland. *Laddie* is what they call boys in Scotland. Locate Scotland on a map or globe and show children photographs of Scotland and of Scottish people wearing kilts. Explain that most of the time, children in Scotland dress the way children in the United States do. However, for a special event children in Scotland might wear a traditional item of Scottish clothing called a kilt, which looks like a skirt.

Pass out the mini-book pages for children to assemble. Have them follow along as you sing the song. Read the text aloud as children look at the illustrations. Ask children to describe what is happening on each page (*children are playing hide-and-seek*).

Activities

♪ Teach children the following game. Have everyone stand in a circle and ask one girl (the "lassie") to stand in the center. As you sing the first half of the song, the lassie in the middle does something silly—makes a face, a movement, and so on. The rest of the class mimics her movements as they sing. When you sing "Did you ever see a laddie…," the lassie chooses a boy to be the laddie and take her place. The laddie then performs silly movements while the class mimics them. Repeat until everyone has had a turn. (Suggest that children choose someone who has not yet had a turn.)

♪ Ask children how the words *lassie* and *laddie* are alike. Can they name other words that begin with /l/? Ask, "What sounds do you hear in the middle of *lassie* and *laddie*?" Say the words slowly and emphasize the medial sound. Ask, "How are the middle sounds different? What sound do you hear at the end of these two words?" Explain that the sound at the end of the words is also the same. Introduce other words slowly, and have children isolate the beginning, middle, and ending sounds.

♪ Lead a movement activity to help children distinguish the position of sounds in words. Explain that you will name a sound, such as /th/. When you say a word (such as *Thursday* or *math*), children should listen for where they hear /th/. If they hear it at the beginning of the word, they should touch their head. If they hear it in the middle of the word, they should touch their stomach. If they hear it at the end, they should touch their toes. You might name several words with the same sound. Repeat with different sounds.

♪ Use children's names as you sing the song—for example, "Did you ever see Maria, Maria…" This is a good activity to help children learn one another's names at the beginning of the year.

♪ Staple a strip of tissue paper to a straw for each child. Demonstrate how to move the streamer in front of your body to make figure eights as you sing the song. Have children take turns performing movements with their streamers while their classmates mirror what they are doing.

Rock-a-Bye, Baby

Purpose
Children develop phonemic awareness by recognizing alliterative and rhyming words.

Directions
Wrap a baby doll in a blanket and begin singing this song as you rock the doll. Ask children why they think people sing to babies. Explain that a lullaby is a song that comforts a baby and helps him or her fall asleep. Ask children to think about what a lullaby might sound like (soft and slow) and what might happen if a lullaby were loud and fast. Would it help a baby to fall sleep? Demonstrate as you sing the song loudly and quickly, rocking the baby to the rhythm of the song. Invite children to pretend they are rocking a baby and sing a lullaby.

Distribute the mini-book pages for students to assemble. Ask children to determine how the words *bye* and *baby* are alike. Have them find and circle these words in their mini-books. Can they name other words that begin with /b/? List these on the chalkboard or chart paper. Ask children how *fall* and *all* are alike. Can they underline the parts of these words that sound alike? Sing the song together as children follow along in their books.

Activities

♪ Discuss the song lyrics. What do students think the words mean? Do they think anyone would hang a baby basket in a tree? Ask children if they can think of other unrealistic examples from songs and nursery rhymes.

♪ Make a class book titled "What to Do When a Baby Cries." Invite each child to draw a picture showing what he or she would do to comfort a crying baby. Then have children dictate a sentence or two describing their illustration. This makes a great gift for a colleague or parent who is expecting a child.

♪ Have each child bring in a baby picture. Attach self-sticking notes with children's names on the backs of the pictures. Then challenge children to guess who is the baby in each picture. Talk about how children have changed since they were babies.

♪ Make "Two Babies in a Bed" for snack. Slice a cooked hot dog in half lengthwise and place the two pieces on a slice of bread. Place a slice of cheese on top of the hot dog pieces so that the tops are still showing, like two babies tucked in a bed. Broil and enjoy. (**Safety Note:** Some children have food allergies or other dietary restrictions. Be sure to obtain a food restriction list from families before proceeding with any food-related activities.)

Old MacDonald

Purpose
Children name the vowels and state their short sounds. Children provide rhyming words.

Directions
In advance, make enlarged copies of the mini-book pages. Color and cut out the animals. Then attach a piece of Velcro to the back of each. As you sing a verse, place the appropriate animal on a flannel board.

Distribute the mini-book pages for children to assemble. Then sing the song together as children point to the animal on each page. You might have a volunteer place animals on the flannel board as the class sings.

Activities

♪ Tell children that you will now teach them a similar song. Begin by prominently displaying or writing the five vowels. Then sing the song below, replacing *Teacher's name* with your own.

Teacher's name had a class.
A-E-I-O-U.
And in this class they had some vowels.
A-E-I-O-U.
With an /a/ /a/ here and an /a/ /a/ there.
Here an /a/, there an /a/,
Everywhere an /a/ /a/.
Teacher's name had a class.
A-E-I-O-U.

Sing one verse for each vowel, using the short-vowel sound. Point to each vowel on the board each time you sing the short-vowel sound. Repeat with long-vowel sounds.

♪ Extend the activity above by singing about objects found in the classroom. Have children take turns suggesting objects that you might mention in a song. For example, if you choose to sing about your desk, the verse might sound like this:

Teacher's name had a desk.
A-E-I-O-U.
And on her desk she had some books.
A-E-I-O-U.
With a book, book here and a book, book there.
Here a book, there a book,
Everywhere a book, book.
Teacher's name had a desk.
A-E-I-O-U.

♪ Read the riddles below and invite children to guess the missing rhyming words. If they find this task difficult, supply the first sound of the missing word, exaggerating if necessary. Then have children name the animal.

I give you milk to drink each day.
Moo, moo is what I ____. (say)

I like to swim and waddle around.
I make a quack, quack, quacking ____. (sound)

Give me milk, and I'll purr, purr, purr.
I have ears, whiskers, and soft, soft, ____. (fur)

Oink-oink is what I say.
In the mud I like to ____. (play)

Baa, baa! I'll give you wool.
I have three bags ____. (full)

Neigh, neigh! Come and play.
Get on my back and ride ____. (away)

I'll woof, woof if you give me a bone.
When I'm your friend, you're never ____. (alone)

♪ Create your own rhyming riddles about objects found in your classroom or school. Invite children to make up their own riddles.

♪ Display the animal pictures on a flannel board and count them together. Have children close their eyes and then remove one animal. After studying the remaining animals, challenge children to guess which animal is missing. Replace the animal and then play again.

♪ Arrange the animals in a specific order on a flannel board. Have children name them in order, then close their eyes. Rearrange one or two. Ask a volunteer to place the animals back in their original order.

♪ Invite children to act as different animals while their classmates guess which animal they're portraying.

♪ Make extra copies of the mini-book. Have children color, cut out, and tape the pictures to craft sticks to make animal puppets. Invite children to use the puppets as props while they sing the song. (You might also have them make paper bag puppets of each animal in the song.)

It's Raining, It's Pouring

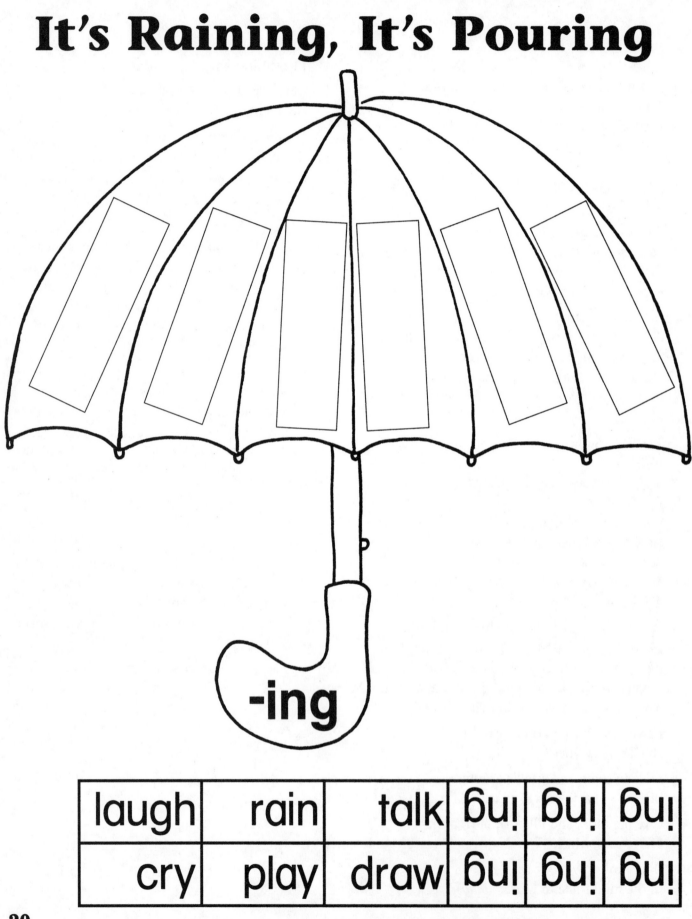

-ing

laugh	rain	talk	ing	ing	ing
cry	play	draw	ing	ing	ing

Teaching Tunes Audio CD and Mini-Books Set: Favorite Songs   Scholastic Professional Books

Yankee Doodle Template

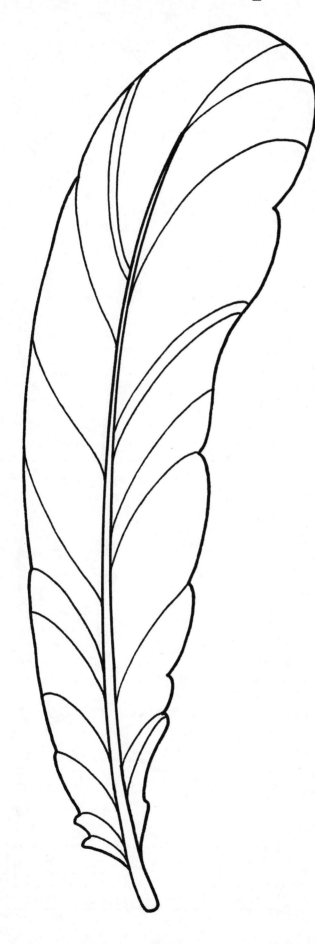

Three Little Kittens Template

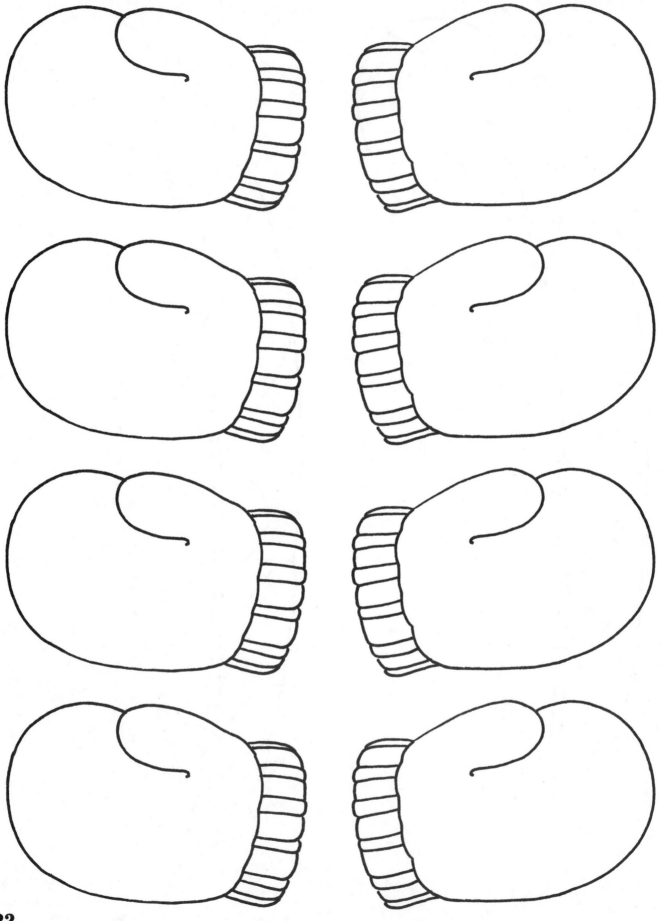

Teaching Tunes Audio CD and Mini-Books Set: Favorite Songs   Scholastic Professional Books

Color the stars, moon, and sky.

8

Teaching Tunes Audio CD and Mini-Books Set: Favorite Songs   Scholastic Professional Books

Twinkle, Twinkle, Little Star

1

Twinkle, twinkle, little star,

6

how I wonder what you are.

3

Twinkle, twinkle, little star,

how I wonder what you are!

Up above the world so high,

like a diamond in the sky.

What kind of muffins do you like to eat?
Draw them in the basket.

The Muffin Man

8

I

the muffin man,
the muffin man.

the muffin man,
the muffin man?

6

3

Do you know the
muffin man,

Yes, we know the
muffin man
who lives in Drury Lane.

Do you know the muffin man
who lives in Drury Lane?

Yes, we know the
muffin man,

How many spiders can you find? Circle the spiders.

8

Teaching Tunes Audio CD and Mini-Books Set: Favorite Songs   Scholastic Professional Books

Itsy Bitsy Spider

1

Out came the sun and dried up all the rain.

6

went up the waterspout.

3

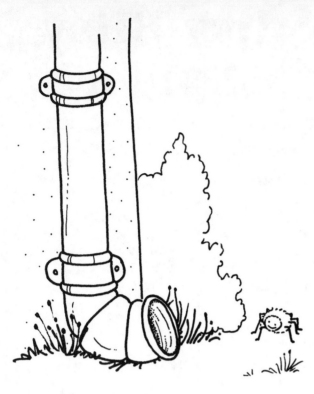

The itsy bitsy spider

And the itsy bitsy spider went up the spout again.

Down came the rain

and washed the spider out.

What do you like to do when it rains? Draw a picture of it.

8

It's Raining, It's Pouring

Teaching Tunes Audio CD and Mini-Books Set: Favorite Songs   Scholastic Professional Books

1

and he bumped his head.

6

It's pouring!

3

It's raining!

And he couldn't get up
in the morning.

The old man is snoring.

He went to bed,

and with the girls be handy.

8

Yankee Doodle

Teaching Tunes Audio CD and Mini-Books Set: Favorite Songs   Scholastic Professional Books

I

Yankee Doodle, keep it up.
Yankee Doodle dandy.

6

a-riding on a pony.

3

Yankee Doodle went to town,

Mind the music and the step,

He stuck a feather in his cap

and called it macaroni.

Draw patterns on the mittens. Then color them.

Three Little Kittens

Teaching Tunes Audio CD and Mini-Books Set: Favorite Songs   Scholastic Professional Books

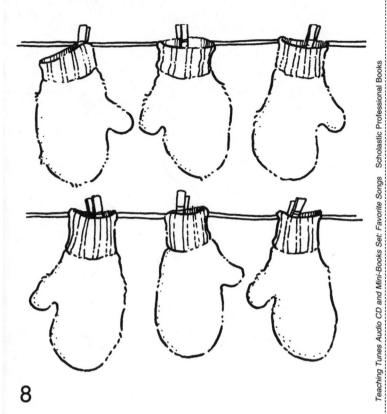

"What, found your mittens?
You darling kittens!
Then you shall have
some pie."

"What, lost your mittens?
You naughty kittens!
Then you shall have no pie."

The three little kittens,
they lost their mittens,
and they began to cry.
"Oh, mother dear,
we sadly fear
our mittens we have lost."

"Meow, meow!
We shall have some pie."

"Meow, meow!
We shall have no pie."

The three little kittens,
they found their mittens
and they began to cry.
"Oh, mother dear,
see here, see here,
our mittens we have found."

What is one of your dreams?
Draw a picture of it.

8

Teaching Tunes Audio CD and Mini-Books Set: Favorite Songs   Scholastic Professional Books

Row, Row, Row Your Boat

1

life is but a dream.

6

gently down the stream.

3

Draw yourself rowing
the boat.

Row, row, row your boat

2

7

Merrily, merrily,

merrily, merrily,

4

5

Draw yourself crossing
London Bridge.

Teaching Tunes Audio CD and Mini-Books Set: Favorite Songs   Scholastic Professional Books

London Bridge

8

1

Build it up with
silver and gold,
silver and gold,
silver and gold.

London Bridge is
falling down,
my fair lady.

6

3

London Bridge is
falling down,
falling down, falling down.

Build it up with
silver and gold,
my fair lady.

Take the key and
lock her up,
lock her up, lock her up.

Take the key and
lock her up,
my fair lady.

we all stand up!

Teaching Tunes Audio CD and Mini-Books Set: Favorite Songs   Scholastic Professional Books

Ring Around the Rosie

Ring around the rosie,
a pocketful of posies.

a pocketful of posies.

Ring around the rosie,

Upstairs, downstairs,

Upstairs, downstairs,

we all fall down!

Can you find the children?
Circle them.

Did You Ever See a Lassie?

Teaching Tunes Audio CD and Mini-Books Set: Favorite Songs   Scholastic Professional Books

8

1

Go this way and that way,
and this way and that way.

Go this way and that way,
and this way and that way.

6

3

Did you ever see a lassie,
a lassie, a lassie?
Did you ever see a lassie
go this way and that?

2

Did you ever see a laddie
go this way and that?

7

Did you ever see a lassie
go this way and that?

4

Did you ever see a laddie,
a laddie, a laddie?
Did you ever see a laddie
go this way and that?

5

What did you look like when you were a baby?
Draw a picture in the frame.

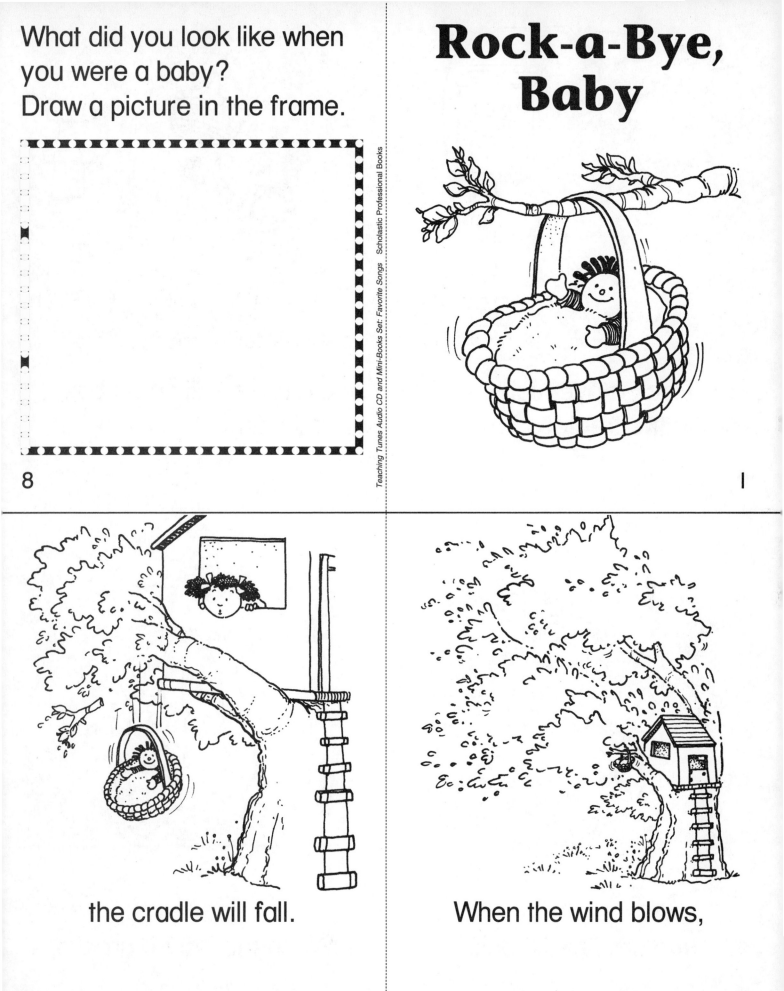

Rock-a-Bye, Baby

Teaching Tunes Audio CD and Mini-Books Set: Favorite Songs   Scholastic Professional Books

8

1

the cradle will fall.

When the wind blows,

6

3

Rock-a-bye, baby
in the treetop.

And down will come baby,
cradle and all.

the cradle will rock.

When the bough breaks,

What is your favorite farm animal? Draw a picture here.

16

Teaching Tunes Audio CD and Mini-Books Set: Favorite Songs   Scholastic Professional Books

Old MacDonald

1

Old MacDonald had a farm.
E-I-E-I-O.
And on this farm he had a dog.
E-I-E-I-O.

14

With a "Moo, moo" here.
And a "Moo, moo" there.
Here a "Moo."
There a "Moo."
Everywhere a "Moo, moo."
Old MacDonald had a farm.
E-I-E-I-O.

3

Old MacDonald had a farm.
E-I-E-I-O.
And on this farm he had
a cow.
E-I-E-I-O.

With a "Woof, woof" here.
And a "Woof, woof" there.
Here a "Woof."
There a "Woof."
Everywhere a "Woof, woof."
Old MacDonald had a farm.
E-I-E-I-O.

Old MacDonald had a farm.
E-I-E-I-O.
And on this farm he had
a pig.
E-I-E-I-O.

With a "Meow, meow" here.
And a "Meow, meow" there.
Here a "Meow."
There a "Meow."
Everywhere a "Meow, meow."
Old MacDonald had a farm.
E-I-E-I-O.

Old MacDonald had a farm.
E-I-E-I-O.
And on this farm he had
a cat.
E-I-E-I-O.

12

Teaching Tunes Audio CD and Mini-Books Set: Favorite Songs   Scholastic Professional Books

With an "Oink, oink" here.
And an "Oink, oink" there.
Here an "Oink."
There an "Oink."
Everywhere an "Oink, oink."
Old MacDonald had a farm.
E-I-E-I-O.

5

Old MacDonald had a farm.
E-I-E-I-O.
And on this farm he had
a duck.
E-I-E-I-O.

10

With a "Baa, baa" here.
And a "Baa, baa" there.
Here a "Baa."
There a "Baa."
Everywhere a "Baa, baa."
Old MacDonald had a farm.
E-I-E-I-O.

7

Old MacDonald had a farm.
E-I-E-I-O.
And on this farm he had
a sheep.
E-I-E-I-O.

With a "Quack, quack" here.
And a "Quack, quack" there.
Here a "Quack."
There a "Quack."
Everywhere a "Quack, quack."
Old MacDonald had a farm.
E-I-E-I-O.

Old MacDonald had a farm.
E-I-E-I-O.
And on this farm he had
a horse.
E-I-E-I-O.

With a "Neigh, neigh" here.
And a "Neigh, neigh" there.
Here a "Neigh."
There a "Neigh."
Everywhere a "Neigh, neigh."
Old MacDonald had a farm.
E-I-E-I-O.